EVOLVE

WORKBOOK

Samuela Eckstut

1A

CAMBRIDGE
UNIVERSITY PRESS

CAMBRIDGE
UNIVERSITY PRESS

University Printing House, Cambridge CB2 8BS, United Kingdom

One Liberty Plaza, 20th Floor, New York, NY 10006, USA

477 Williamstown Road, Port Melbourne, VIC 3207, Australia

314–321, 3rd Floor, Plot 3, Splendor Forum, Jasola District Centre, New Delhi – 110025, India

103 Penang Road, #05-06/07, Visioncrest Commercial, Singapore 238467

Cambridge University Press is part of the University of Cambridge.

It furthers the University's mission by disseminating knowledge in the pursuit of education, learning and research at the highest international levels of excellence.

www.cambridge.org
Information on this title: www.cambridge.org/9781108408592

First published 2019

20 19 18 17 16 15 14 13 12 11 10 9 8

Printed in Poland by Opolgraf

A catalogue record for this publication is available from the British Library

ISBN 978-1-108-40521-8 Student's Book
ISBN 978-1-108-40503-4 Student's Book A
ISBN 978-1-108-40914-8 Student's Book B
ISBN 978-1-108-40522-5 Student's Book with Practice Extra
ISBN 978-1-108-40504-1 Student's Book with Practice Extra A
ISBN 978-1-108-40915-5 Student's Book with Practice Extra B
ISBN 978-1-108-40894-3 Workbook with Audio
ISBN 978-1-108-40859-2 Workbook with Audio A
ISBN 978-1-108-41191-2 Workbook with Audio B
ISBN 978-1-108-40512-6 Teacher's Edition with Test Generator
ISBN 978-1-108-41062-5 Presentation Plus
ISBN 978-1-108-41201-8 Class Audio CDs
ISBN 978-1-108-40791-5 Video Resource Book with DVD
ISBN 978-1-108-41200-1 Full Contact with DVD
ISBN 978-1-108-41152-3 Full Contact with DVD A
ISBN 978-1-108-41410-4 Full Contact with DVD B

Additional resources for this publication at www.cambridge.org/evolve

CONTENTS

UNIT 1 I AM ...

1.1 I'M BRAZILIAN. AND YOU?

1 VOCABULARY: Countries and nationalities

A **Read and complete the sentences.**

1 I'm ___Peruvian___. I'm from Lima in Peru.
2 I'm Japanese. I'm from Tokyo in ___Japan___.
3 I'm from Tegucigalpa in ______________. I'm Honduran.
4 I'm ______________. I'm from Madrid in Spain.
5 I'm from Medellín in ______________. I'm Colombian.
6 I'm ______________. I'm from Rio de Janeiro in Brazil.
7 I'm from Beijing in ______________. I'm Chinese.
8 I'm ______________. I'm from Moscow in Russia.
9 I'm from Miami in ______________. I'm American.
10 I'm from Seoul in South Korea. I'm ______________.
11 I'm ______________. I'm from Santiago in Chile.
12 I'm ______________. I'm from Mexico City in Mexico.
13 I'm from Quito in Ecuador. I'm ______________.
14 I'm ______________. I'm from Paris in France.

2 GRAMMAR: *I am, you are*

A **Circle the correct words.**

1 I (*am*) / *are* Mexican.
2 *Am* / *Are* you from Russia?
3 *Am* / *Are* you María?
4 No, I *'m* / *'re* Diana.
5 You *'m* / *'re* not Ivan.
6 Yes, I *'m* / *'re* in Seoul!

B **Complete the conversation. Use the words in the box.**

'm	are	~~are you~~	I am
I'm	I'm not	you	you're

Tony [1] ___Are you___ Ana?
Ana Yes, [2] ________.
Tony Hi, [3] ________ Tony. I'm from Lima.
Ana Oh, [4] ________ Peruvian. I [5] ________ Brazilian.
Tony [6] ________ you from Rio?
Ana No, [7] ________. I'm not from Rio or São Paulo.
Tony Are [8] ________ from Brasília?
Ana Yes.

3 GRAMMAR AND VOCABULARY

A **Write true sentences for you.**

1 teacher ___I'm not a teacher.___
2 student ___I'm a student.___
3 Mexico City ________
4 American ________
5 Alex ________
6 Chile ________

FIND IT

B **Think of three famous people. Write affirmative (+) and negative (–) sentences.**

Lionel Messi Hi. I'm Lionel Messi. I'm not from Spain. I'm Argentinian.

Michelle Obama Hi. I'm Michelle Obama. I'm American. I'm not from Washington, D.C. I'm from Chicago.

1.2 WHAT'S YOUR LAST NAME?

1 VOCABULARY: The alphabet; personal information

A 1.01 **Listen and write the words the speakers spell.**

1 Palmira
2 ______
3 ______
4 ______
5 ______

B **Match 1–5 with a–e.**

1 Harvard University d
2 Toyota ______
3 tonyravella@mymail.org ______
4 Ravella ______
5 Tony ______

a email address
b first name
c company
d college
e last name

C **Make sentences with the words from exercise 1B.**

1 My college is Harvard University.
2 ______
3 ______
4 ______
5 ______

2 GRAMMAR: *What's . . . ? It's . . .*

A **Read 1–6. Check (✓) *Question* or *Answer*.**

	Question	Answer
1 What's your first name?	✓	
2 It's Nippon College.		
3 What's the name of your company?		
4 What's your last name?		
5 It's Higuera.		
6 It's cccomputers@mymail.org.		

B **Complete the questions and answers.**

1 ________ your first name? ________ Mike.

2 ________ your last name? ________ Ramirez.

3 ________ the name of your ________? It's Nippon College.

3 GRAMMAR AND VOCABULARY

A **Find and correct <u>three</u> mistakes in the conversation.**

Anna Hello. What your last name?

Mike It's Lugo. L-U-G-O.

Anna Uh-huh. What's your first name?

Mike It Mike.

Anna And what's your email address?

Mike Its mikelugo@mymail.org.

B **Answer the questions for you.**

1 What's your last name? ________

2 What's your first name? ________

3 What's your email address? ________

1.3 THIS IS THE KEY

1 FUNCTIONAL LANGUAGE: Checking into a hotel

A **Complete the conversation. Use the words in the box.**

cell phone number	It's	last	nights	room
sign	This is	~~Welcome~~	what's	

Clerk Hello. [1] *Welcome* to the Capital Hotel.
Anna Hello. I'm Anna. I'm here for two [2] ________.
Clerk What's your [3] ________ name, Anna?
Anna It's Wang. W-A-N-G.
Clerk Ah, yes. Anna Wang. What's your [4] ________, Anna?
Anna It's (243) 555–1968.
Clerk And [5] ________ your email address?
Anna [6] ________ wang99@mymail.org.
Clerk Thank you. One moment. Please [7] ________ here.
Anna OK.
Clerk [8] ________ the key. You're in [9] ________ 10F.
Anna Great. Thank you.
Clerk You're welcome.

2 REAL-WORLD STRATEGY: Checking spelling

A **Dan is at a hotel. The clerk asks about spelling. Write the questions.**

1 **Dan** I'm Dan Gonzales.
Clerk ________
Dan G-O-N-Z-A-L-E-S.

2 **Dan** My email address is dgonza14@mail.org.
Clerk ________
Dan D-G-O-N-Z-A-14 at M-A-I-L dot O-R-G.

3 **Dan** I'm from Martin Hotel Company.
Clerk ________
Dan M-A-R-T-I-N.

3 FUNCTIONAL LANGUAGE AND REAL-WORLD STRATEGY

A **Read the sentences. Who says each sentence? Check (✓) the correct column.**

	A hotel clerk	A hotel guest	A hotel clerk OR a hotel guest
1 Hello.			✓
2 Welcome to City Hotel.			
3 What's your name?			
4 How do you spell your last name?			
5 I'm here for one night.			
6 What's your cell phone number?			
7 Here's the key.			
8 You're in room 316.			
9 Thank you.			
10 You're welcome.			
11 My name is Robert Dupont.			

B **Write a conversation between a hotel clerk and a hotel guest. Use the sentences in exercise 3A and the conversations on page 6 to help you. Add <u>one</u> question from the hotel clerk.**

1.4 MY PROFILE

1 VOCABULARY: Jobs

A **Look at the pictures and read the conversations. Circle an answer (*a* or *b*). Write the correct job in *b*.**

1 Are you a salesperson?
   a Yes, I am.
   b No, I'm not. I'm a ________________.

2 Are you an artist?
   a Yes, I am.
   b No, I'm not. I'm a ________________.

3 Are you a teacher?
   a Yes, I am.
   b No, I'm not. I'm a ________________.

4 Are you a hotel clerk?
   a Yes, I am.
   b No, I'm not. I'm a ________________.

2 READING

A READ FOR DETAILS **Read the profile. Check (✓) the information in the profile.**

My name is David Pérez Delgado. David is my first name. Pérez and Delgado are my last names. In the United States my last name is Pérez. I'm a salesperson in Mexico. I'm from Mexico City. I'm an English student at a school in Texas. The name of the school is Texas International Language School. My teacher is from Austin, Texas. She is American.

1 nationality ______
2 last name ______
3 email address ______
4 job in Mexico ______
5 the name of the English school ______
6 the name of the English teacher ______

3 WRITING

A **Complete the conversations. Use *Hello, Hi,* or *Hey.***

1	**Teacher**	______	My name is Mr. Hewson. You're new here.
	Student	______	Yes. I'm a new student. My name is Yasuhiro Momoto.
2	**Student**	______	Yasu. How are you? Are you a student here?
	Student	______	Jaime. Yes, I am. How are you?

B **Change the sentences. Use capital letters and periods.**

1 i'm emma durand — I'm Emma Durand.
2 i'm a french chef ______
3 my home is in new york ______
4 i'm from paris in france ______
5 i'm french and american ______
6 i'm a teacher ______
7 the name of the school is new york chef school ______
8 my students are from the united states, canada, mexico, and japan ______

C **How are you and Emma Durand different? Write four sentences.**

I'm not Emma Durand. I'm Lisa Santiago.

______

______

______

______

CHECK AND REVIEW

Read the statements. Can you do these things?

UNIT 1	Mark the boxes. ☑ I can do it. ? I am not sure. **I can …**	If you are not sure, go back to these pages in the Student's Book.
VOCABULARY	☐ **use words for countries and nationalities.**	page 2
	☐ **use the alphabet.**	page 5
	☐ **use words for personal information.**	page 5
	☐ **use words for numbers.**	page 6
	☐ **use words for jobs.**	page 8
GRAMMAR	☐ **use *I am* and *you are*.**	page 3
	☐ **ask and answer questions with *What's … ?* and *It's …***	page 5
FUNCTIONAL LANGUAGE	☐ **check into a hotel.**	page 6
	☐ **check spelling.**	page 7
SKILLS	☐ **write a personal profile.**	page 9
	☐ **use capital letters and periods.**	page 9

UNIT 2 GREAT PEOPLE

2.1 A FAMILY PARTY

1 VOCABULARY: Family; numbers

A **You are Bill. Look at the family tree. Then write the family words in 2–12.**

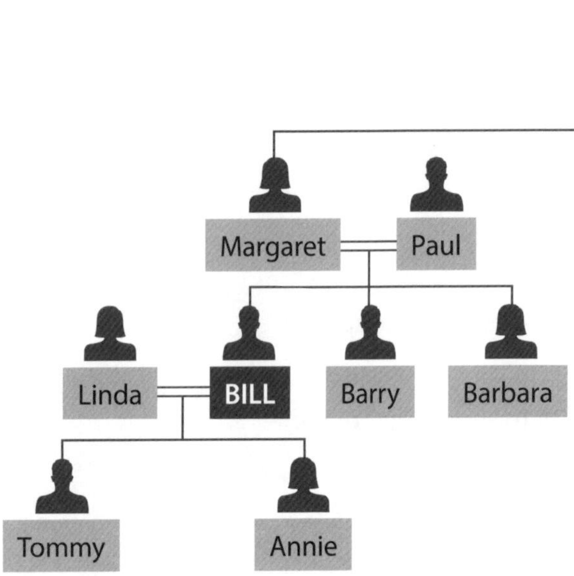

aunt	brother	children
daughter	~~father~~	grandfather
grandmother	mother	sister
son	uncle	wife

1 Paul is my *father*.
2 Helen is my ________.
3 Barry is my ________.
4 Tommy and Annie are my ________.
5 Barbara is my ________.
6 Linda is my ________.
7 Tommy is my ________.
8 Annie is my ________.
9 Anna is my ________.
10 John is my ________.
11 Margaret is my ________.
12 Peter is my ________.

B **Match the numbers and words.**

13 sixty-five 18 eleven 47 seventy-one 16 eighteen fifteen

one hundred twenty-four 82 fourteen 19 60 twenty-nine

fifty-five 94 88 30 ten 55 29 70 50 sixty

forty-six 65 eighty-two forty-seven ninety-three 46 thirty-nine

ninety-four thirteen thirty 100 15 93 eighty-eight 11 twelve

seventy sixteen fifty nineteen 12 24 71 10 39 14

2 GRAMMAR: *is / are* in statements and *yes/no* questions

A **Complete the sentences with *is* or *are*.**

Hello. My name [1] ___is___ Tamara. My family and I [2] ________ Colombian. We [3] ________ from Bogotá. My grandparents [4] ________ from Medellín. My father [5] ________ a teacher, and my mother [6] ________ an artist. My brothers [7] ________ 19 and 14. My sister [8] ________ 21. My sister and I [9] ________ college students.

B **Write questions and answers about Tamara. Use the words in parentheses ( ).**

1 (your name / Rosaria) Is your name Rosaria?
No, it isn't. It's Tamara.

2 (you and your family / Colombian) ________
____

3 (you / from Medellín) ________
____

4 (your grandparents / from Medellín) ________
____

5 (your father / an artist) ________
____

6 (your sister / 21) ________
____

C **Write two more questions about Tamara.**

1 ________
2 ________

3 GRAMMAR AND VOCABULARY

A **Read the answers. Write questions about <u>your</u> family.**

1 Is your mother American? No, she's not.
2 Are your cousins here? No, they're not.
3 ________ Yes, he is.
4 ________ Yes, she is.
5 ________ Yes, we are.
6 ________ Yes, they are.
7 ________ No, we're not.
8 ________ No, he's not.

2.2 THEY'RE REALLY FUNNY!

1 VOCABULARY: Describing people; *really / very*

A **Write the correct adjectives from the box for the pictures.**

boring	friendly	funny	interesting	~~old~~
short	shy	smart	tall	young

1 *old*

2 ______

3 ______

4 ______

5 ______

6 ______

7 ______

8 ______

9 ______

10 ______

B **Circle the correct answer.**

1

a Her husband is tall.

b Her husband is really tall.

c Her husband isn't very tall.

2

a Nicolas is boring.

b Nicolas is really boring.

c Nicolas isn't very boring.

3

a My brother isn't very shy.

b My brother isn't shy.

c My brother is very shy.

4

a Celia is smart.

b Celia isn't smart.

c Celia isn't very smart.

2 GRAMMAR: *is not / are not*

A **Complete the sentences. Use *'s, is, 're, are,* or *isn't, aren't* or *not*.**

1 Sachi is from Los Angeles. She's not from Peru.
2 My uncle's not very interesting. ________ boring.
3 My brother and I are in college. ________ very smart.
4 He ________ really tall, but I'm short.
5 My children are 2 and 4. ________ very old.
6 Joe is my dog. ________ really friendly!

B **Write the sentences again. Use *'s not, isn't, 're not,* and *aren't*.**

1 You are not boring. You are funny.
You're not boring. You're funny!
2 My sister is not tall, and she is not old. She is five.
____
3 My husband and I are not from Mexico, and we are not from Canada. We are from the United States.
____
4 Mr. May is not my teacher, and he is not your teacher. He is the chef at our school.
____
5 Dr. Norton is not here, and she is not at home. She is at the college.
____
6 Rita and Lara are not sisters, and they are not cousins. They are friends.
____

3 GRAMMAR AND VOCABULARY

A **Write true sentences. Use the words in the box.**

My parents	is	really	boring
My mother	isn't	very	friendly
My father	are		funny
My grandparents	aren't		interesting
My cousins			old
My sister			short
My brother			shy
My best friend			smart
My teacher			tall
			young

1 My mother isn't very tall. My father is tall.
2 ________
3 ________
4 ________
5 ________
6 ________
7 ________
8 ________
9 ________

2.3 WHEN IS YOUR BIRTHDAY?

1 FUNCTIONAL LANGUAGE: Asking about and saying ages and birthdays

A **Read the sentences (a–h). Then write a conversation for Diego, Anna, and Sophia.**

a Happy birthday, Diego!
b Oh, right! You're seven this month? Happy birthday from me!
c Oh, wow! When is your birthday, Sophia?
d Thanks. Oh, Anna. This is my daughter, Sophia.
e I'm six, and my brother is three years old.
f ~~Today is my birthday.~~
g Hello, Sophia. My name is Anna. How old are you?
h It's on December 5.

Diego Today is my birthday.
Anna ______
Diego ______
Anna ______
Sophia ______
Anna ______
Sophia ______
Anna ______

B **Look at the underlined numbers. Write the words.**

1 He's 4. four — His birthday is February 4. fourth
2 She's 30. ______ — Her birthday is April 30. ______
3 He's 1. ______ — His birthday is January 1. ______
4 She's 22. ______ — Her birthday is March 22. ______
5 I'm 31. ______ — My birthday is July 31. ______
6 She's 3. ______ — Her birthday is June 3. ______
7 He's 27. ______ — His birthday is May 27. ______
8 She's 18. ______ — Her birthday is August 18. ______

2 REAL-WORLD STRATEGY: Correcting yourself

A **Read the sentences. Correct the mistakes with information in the box. Use *No, sorry,* or *Sorry, I mean*.**

Alexa—12, March 2	Cecilia—15, May 30
Sandra—19, April 30	Ariana—21, September 13

1 It's my sister Alexa's birthday today. She's 13.
No, sorry, 12.
2 My sister Cecilia is 15. Her birthday is April 30.
______
3 My sister Sandra's birthday is April 30. She's 17.
______
4 Ariana is 21. Her birthday is November 13.
______

3 FUNCTIONAL LANGUAGE AND REAL-WORLD STRATEGY

A **Use the words in the box to complete the conversation.**

mean old sorry when years

Paul This is my niece, Olivia.
Gabriela Hi, Olivia! How [1] ______ are you?
Olivia I'm 10. Sorry, I [2] ______ nine. I'm nine years and eleven months old.
Gabriela You're a tall girl! [3] ______ is your birthday?
Olivia It's June 31.
Gabriela June 31?
Olivia No, [4] ______, July 31.
Gabriela Oh. So you're 9 [5] ______ old, and your birthday is July 31.

B **Write a conversation between you and Gabriela about the ages of people in your family.**

Gabriela My brother is 18 years old.
You ______
Gabriela ______
You ______
Gabriela ______
You ______
Gabriela ______
You ______

2.4 HERE'S MY BAND

1 LISTENING

A 2.01 LISTEN FOR GIST **What do the people do together?**

____

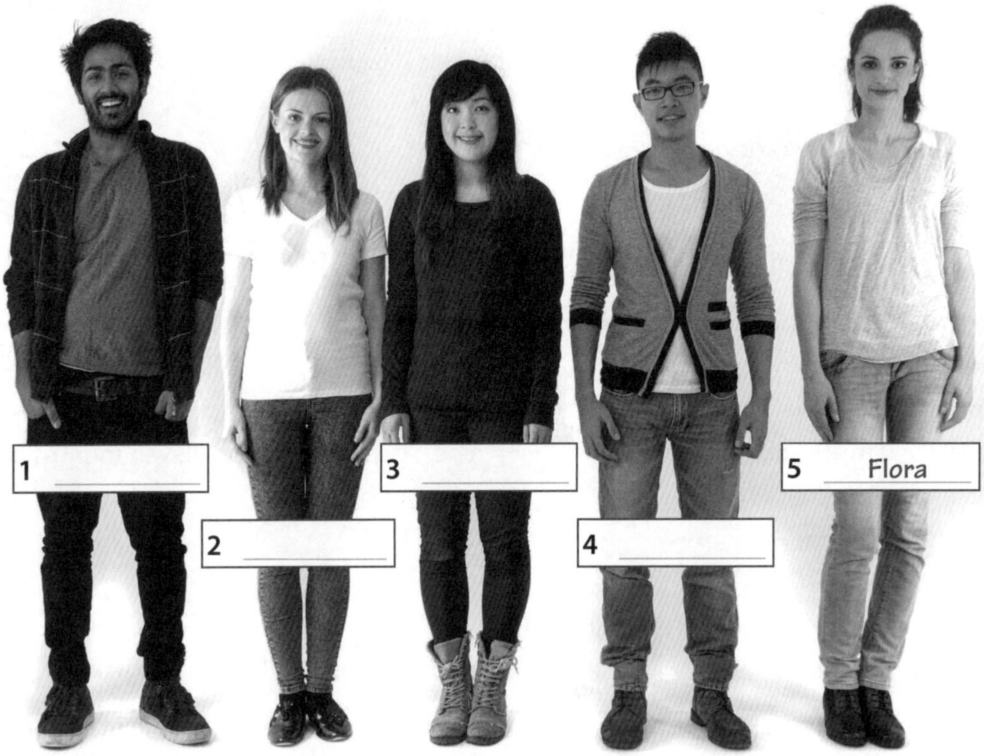

B 2.01 LISTEN FOR DETAIL **Write the names of the people in the photo: *Aniko, Tony, Claudia,* and *Zack*.**

C 2.01 LISTEN FOR DETAIL **Complete the sentences with names from the photo.**

1 ___Zack___ is 23.
2 __________ is from Los Angeles.
3 __________ is an artist.
4 __________ is really friendly.
5 __________ is a doctor.
6 __________ is 28.

2 GRAMMAR: Prepositions of place

A **Read the sentences about the picture in exercise 1. Circle the correct words.**

1 Aniko is *between / on the right* Claudia and Zack.
2 Tony is *in / on* the left.
3 Claudia is *next / next to* Tony.
4 We're *at / in* Chicago.
5 Flora isn't next to *I / me*.

3 WRITING

A **Read the sentences. Underline *and* when it joins words. Circle *and* when it joins sentences.**

1 We are from different countries, (and) we are different ages.
2 Jiyoung and I are from South Korea.
3 Three students are 19, and eight students are 20.
4 Klaus is from Germany, and he is a chef.
5 Klaus is between Jiyoung and me.
6 The teacher is interesting and funny.

B **Read about the people. Join four sentences. Use *and*.**

My friends and I are from different countries. We are different ages. I am from France. Jiyoung and Jinho are from South Korea. One friend is from China. Two friends are from Brazil. Yi is from China. Yi and I are artists. I'm 22. Yi is 24.

1 My friends and I are from different countries, and we are different ages.
2 ______
3 ______
4 ______
5 ______

C **Write about three people in your class. How old are they? Who is: next to you, on the left, on the right, and between you and another student? Use *and* to join words and sentences.**

CHECK AND REVIEW

Read the statements. Can you do these things?

UNIT 2	Mark the boxes. ☑ I can do it. ? I am not sure. **I can …**	If you are not sure, go back to these pages in the Student's Book.
VOCABULARY	☐ **use words for family members.**	page 12
	☐ **say numbers.**	page 12
	☐ **use adjectives to describe people.**	page 14
	☐ **use *really* and *very*.**	page 14
GRAMMAR	☐ **use *is* and *are* in statements and *yes/no* questions.**	page 13
	☐ **use *is not* and *are not*.**	page 15
	☐ **use prepositions of place.**	page 18
FUNCTIONAL LANGUAGE	☐ **ask about and say people's ages and birthdays.**	page 16
	☐ **correct myself.**	page 17
SKILLS	☐ **write a description of the people in my class.**	page 19
	☐ **use *and* to connect words and sentences.**	page 19

3.1 WELCOME TO MY HOME

1 VOCABULARY: Rooms in a home

A **Look at the apartment plan and read the words. Then correct the mistakes in sentences 2–10 below.**

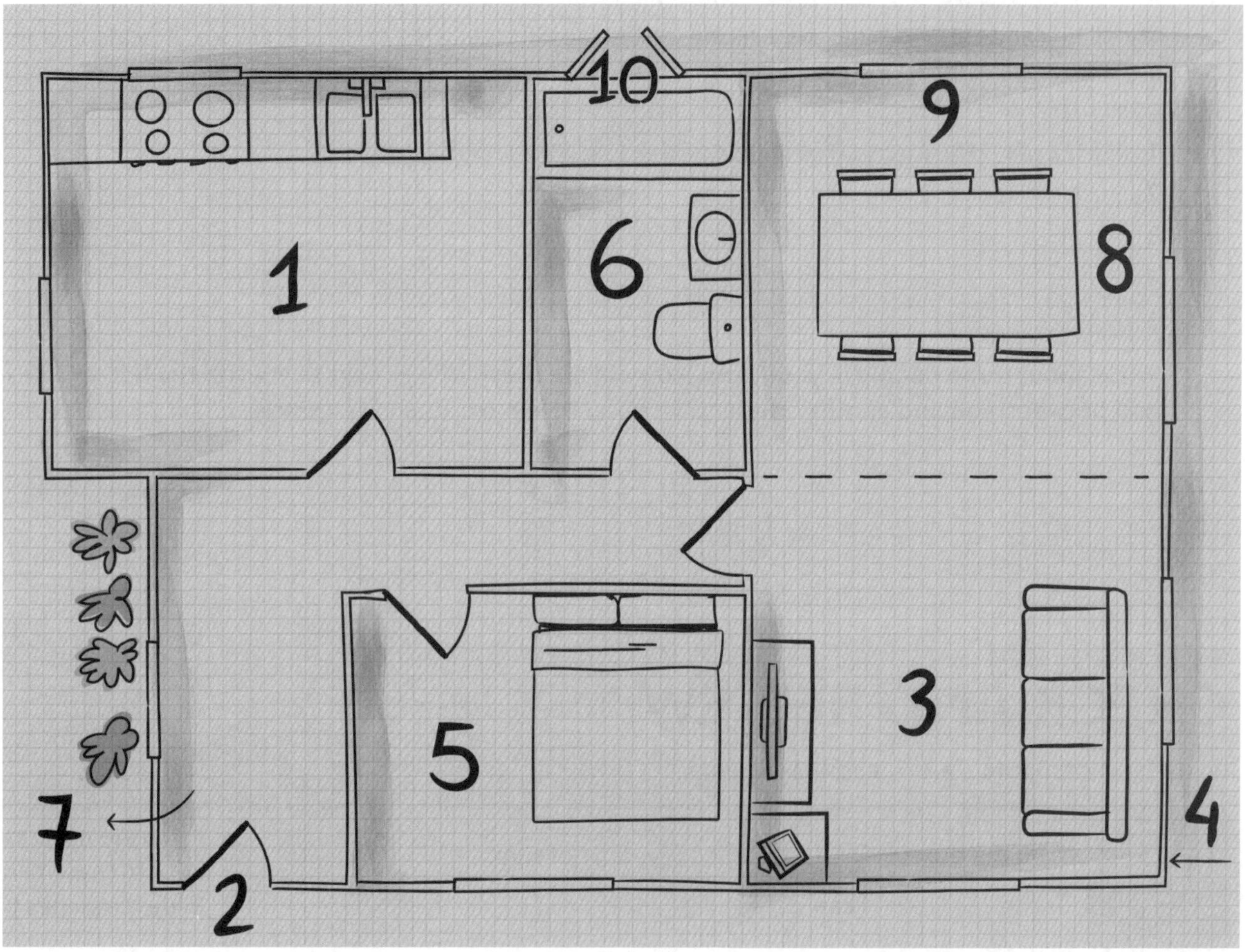

1 This is the living room. *No, it's the kitchen.*
2 This is the floor. ______
3 This is the dining area. ______
4 This is a picture. ______
5 This is a bathroom. ______
6 This is a bedroom. ______
7 This is the door. ______
8 This is the kitchen. ______
9 This is a window. ______
10 This is a wall. ______

2 GRAMMAR: Possessive adjectives; possessive *'s* and *s'*

A **Circle the correct words.**

1 I'm Mr. Costa. *My* / *His* / *Your* first name is Ricardo.
2 We are from Mexico. *Your* / *Their* / *Our* home is in Oaxaca.
3 My cousins are artists. These are *my* / *their* / *his* pictures.
4 Johann has three children. That's *his* / *your* / *her* daughter.
5 Are you married? Where is *your* / *my* / *his* wife?
6 Ms. Montero is an art teacher. *Her* / *My* / *Your* class is in Room 116.

B **Complete the sentences with possessive words.**

1 My parents sleep in this room. It's __my parents'__ bedroom.
2 Jonathan lives in this house. It's ________ house.
3 Her aunt has a picture on the wall. It's her ________ picture.
4 The students have eight books. They are the ________ books.
5 Her cousins have a friendly dog. That's her ________ dog.
6 Sari has a new email address. What's ________ email address?

3 GRAMMAR AND VOCABULARY

A **Write sentences about your home or your friends' homes. Use the words in parentheses ( ).**

1 (bedroom / big) __My bedroom is big. OR My bedroom isn't big.__
2 (dining area / next to) ________
3 (kitchen / new) ________
4 (picture / interesting) ________
5 (living room / small) ________
6 (bathroom / between) ________

3.2 IS IT REALLY A CHAIR?

1 VOCABULARY: Furniture

A **Look at the letters in A. Write the furniture in B. Write the name of the room in C.**

	A Letters	B Furniture	C Room / Rooms
1	sked	desk	living room or bedroom
2	koobseac		
3	niks		
4	gur		
5	hersow		
6	VT		
7	malp		
8	ebd		
9	irach		
10	bleat		
11	gerretirfoar		
12	ochuc		

2 GRAMMAR: *It is*

A **Look at the pictures. Complete the sentences. Use *'s*, *is*, *isn't*, *it's*, or *it's not*.**

1 The bookcase ___isn't___ in the living room. ___It's___ in the dining area.
2 The lamp ________ in the bedroom. ________ in the living room.
3 The TV ________ in the bedroom. ________ in the kitchen.
4 The couch ________ in the living room. ________ in the bedroom.
5 ________ the table in the kitchen? No, ________ in the dining area.
6 ________ the bed in the bedroom? Yes, ________ in the bedroom.

B **Complete the conversation. Use *is, isn't, it's, it is, it's not*, or *is it …?***

Lucy This is our home. [1] ___It's___ in Toronto.

Hyun [2] ______ an apartment?

Lucy No, [3] ______. [4] ______ a house.

Hyun [5] ______ big?

Lucy No. [6] ______ small.

Hyun [7] ______ new?

Lucy Yes, [8] ______. And it's very nice. Is your home in Seoul?

Hyun My home [9] ______ in Seoul. It's in Busan. And [10] ______ an apartment, not a house. The apartment [11] ______ very big, but our small apartment is OK.

3 GRAMMAR AND VOCABULARY

A **Read the words in the boxes. Then make sentences about your home.**

Furniture

bed	bookcase	chair	couch	desk	lamp
refrigerator	rug	shower	sink	table	TV

Rooms

bathroom	bedroom	dining area	kitchen	living room

Adjectives

big	cool	good	great	new
nice	old	short	small	tall

1 *The desk in my bedroom isn't very old.*
2 ______
3 ______
4 ______
5 ______
6 ______
7 ______
8 ______
9 ______
10 ______

3.3 COFFEE OR TEA?

1 FUNCTIONAL LANGUAGE: Making and replying to offers; accepting a drink and snack

A **Look at what Dan, Coco, and Dalia want. Then write the conversations below. Use the words in the box.**

Dan tea, sugar (1), cookie

Coco coffee

Dalia tea, sugar (2), milk, cookie

cookie	coffee	tea	milk	sugar

1

You *Coffee or tea?*
Dan *Tea, please.*
You *With milk?*
Dan *No, thanks.*
You *With sugar?*
Dan *Sure. One, please.*
You *A cookie?*
Dan *Yes, please.*
You *Here you are.*
Dan *Thank you.*

2

You *Coffee or tea?*
Coco *Coffee, please.*
You *With milk?*
Coco ______
You *Sugar?*
Coco ______
You *A cookie?*
Coco ______
You *Here you are.*
Coco ______

3

You *Coffee or tea?*
Dalia ______
You ______
Dalia ______
You ______
Dalia ______
You ______
Dalia ______
You ______
Dalia ______

2 REAL-WORLD STRATEGY: Asking about words you don't understand

A 3.01 **Listen to the conversation. Then check (✓) *True* or *False*.**

	True	False
1 Jason wants coffee.	☐	☐
2 Jason wants milk.	☐	☐
3 Jason wants sugar.	☐	☐
4 Jason understands *biscuit*.	☐	☐
5 Jason wants a cookie.	☐	☐

3 FUNCTIONAL LANGUAGE AND REAL-WORLD STRATEGY

A **Correct the four mistakes in the conversation.**

Lina Coffee or tea?
Jason ~~Tea.~~ *Tea, please.*
Lina With milk?
Jason Yes.
Lina Sugar?
Jason No.
Lina And a biscuit?
Jason Biscuit?
Lina A biscuit is a cookie.
Jason Oh, a cookie. Sure, please.

3.4 HOME-SHARE

1 READING

A **Read about vacation home-shares. Is each home good for two people or for a family (parents + two or three children)? Check (✓) the box.**

1 ☐ Two people ☐ Family

$65, center of Rio de Janeiro

This is a great apartment for one or two weeks. The bedroom is small, but the bed is big. The couch in the living room is a good bed for a child. The living room has a big bookcase and cool pictures on the walls. It has interesting books about Brazil. The kitchen is big and has a table and four chairs. The apartment is a great place to stay. – MATT

2 ☐ Two people ☐ Family

$110, Lapa, Rio de Janeiro

This home is in Lapa, in Rio de Janeiro. The bedrooms in the home are great. One bedroom is big and has a big bed. The second bedroom has two beds. The third bedroom is small and has a small bed. It's good for a child. The apartment has two bathrooms! The showers are great. The kitchen is nice, but the refrigerator is small. It's a good place for four or five days. – KARA

B **Read about the homes again. Check (✓) the things in the homes.**

	Center of Rio de Janeiro	Lapa, Rio de Janeiro
1 bathroom		
2 bedroom		
3 dining area		
4 kitchen		
5 living room		
6 bookcase		
7 desk		
8 picture		
9 shower		
10 television		

2 GRAMMAR: Information questions with *be*

A **Match the question words and answers.**

1 What? ____ a six years old
2 Where? ____ b five
3 How old? ____ c Maria Santos
4 Who? ____ d Rio de Janeiro
5 How many rooms? ____ e myb@xyzmail.com

B **Write the questions and answers from exercise 2A.**

1 (your email address) A *What is your email address?*
B *It's myb@xyzmail.com*

2 (the apartment) A ______
B ______

3 (old/apartment) A ______
B ______

4 (owner) A ______
B ______

5 (rooms) A ______
B ______

3 WRITING

A **Underline the five questions in the email. Change the periods to question marks.**

Reply Forward

Dear Ms. Santos,

This email is about your apartment. Our son is six years old. How many bedrooms are in your apartment. Where is your apartment. What is the name of the street. In your apartment, are pets OK. Our dog is small. Is the TV in the living room.

Thank you.

Sincerely,

Rose Chu

B **Is the email in exercise 3A formal or informal?**

C **You go to a new city for one week. Write an email to the owner of a home-share. Ask questions.**

CHECK AND REVIEW

Read the statements. Can you do these things?

UNIT 3	Mark the boxes. ☑ I can do it. ? I am not sure. **I can …**	If you are not sure, go back to these pages in the Student's Book.
VOCABULARY	☐ **use words for rooms in my home.**	page 22
	☐ **use words for furniture.**	page 24
	☐ **use words for drinks and snacks.**	page 26
GRAMMAR	☐ **use possessive adjectives, *'s*, and *s'*.**	page 23
	☐ **use *it is*.**	page 25
	☐ **ask questions with *be* for information.**	page 28
FUNCTIONAL LANGUAGE	☐ **make and reply to offers.**	page 26
	☐ **ask about words I don't understand.**	page 27
SKILLS	☐ **write an email about a vacation home.**	page 29
	☐ **use question marks.**	page 29

UNIT 4 I LOVE IT

4.1 FAVORITE THINGS

1 VOCABULARY: Technology

A **Find the words in the box in the word search.**

app	camera	~~cell phone~~	earphones
game	laptop	tablet	smartwatch

L	A	P	T	O	P	T	D	W	Z	T
Z	N	B	C	J	G	A	M	E	Q	A
J	K	Y	A	C	K	E	I	K	B	B
M	G	V	M	A	T	Z	I	K	H	L
R	Y	C	E	L	L	P	H	O	N	E
K	E	O	R	T	O	P	Z	A	M	T
A	P	L	A	S	E	T	Y	T	N	P
E	E	A	R	P	H	O	N	E	S	X
A	P	P	M	F	S	Z	N	R	V	K
F	S	M	A	R	T	W	A	T	C	H

B **Write the correct word to match each picture. Use the words in the box in exercise 1A.**

1 ______________

2 ______________

3 *cell phone*

4 ______________

5 ______________

6 ______________

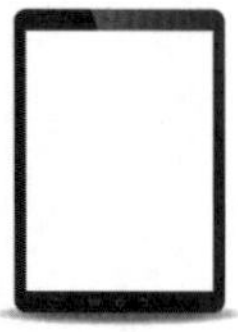

7 ______________

8 ______________

2 GRAMMAR: Simple present statements with *I*, *you*, and *we*

A **Write affirmative (+) and negative (–) statements.**

1 I / not have / a laptop // have / a tablet — *I don't have a laptop. I have a tablet.*
2 I like apps // not like / video games ______________
3 you / want / a small refrigerator // not want / a big refrigerator ______________
4 I / love / photo apps // not love / music apps ______________
5 we / have / an apartment // not have / a house ______________
6 we / not want / a new camera // want / a new computer ______________

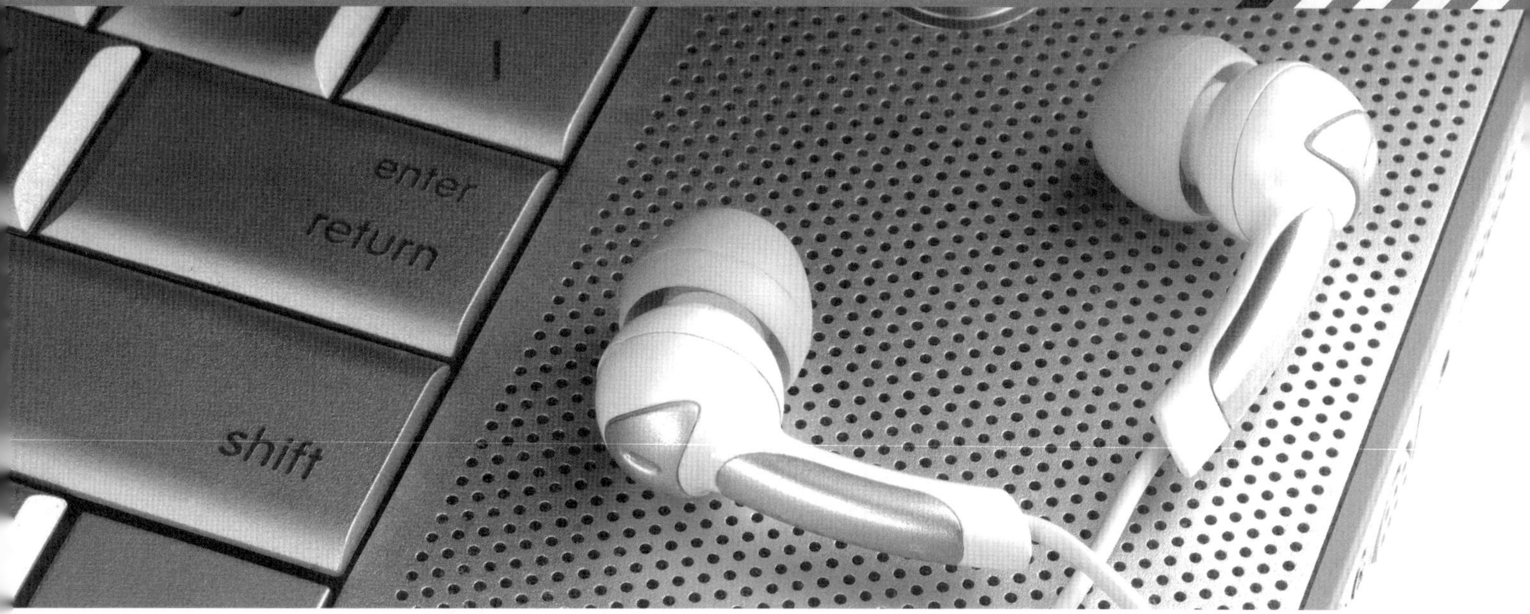

B **Write affirmative (+) and negative (–) sentences. Use the verbs in the box. Start the sentences with *I* or *We*.**

have	like	love	want

1 *We have a new apartment. We don't have a new couch.*
2
3
4
5

3 GRAMMAR AND VOCABULARY

A **Write sentences that are true for you. Then add more information.**

1 love video games
I love video games. I have games on my phone.
OR
I don't love video games. I don't have games on my phone.
2 have cool apps on my phone
3 like earphones
4 want a new tablet
5 have an old laptop
6 love my cell phone
7 want a smartwatch
8 like the camera on my phone

4.2 MY PHONE IS MY WORLD

1 VOCABULARY: Using technology

A **Look at the verbs (1–9). Which <u>two</u> words go after each verb? Circle the correct answers.**

1	call	**a** a game	(b)	a company	(c)	my cousin
2	chat with	**a** my best friend	**b**	my couch	**c**	my sister
3	listen to	**a** my desk	**b**	music	**c**	my teacher
4	post	**a** apps	**b**	messages	**c**	photos
5	read	**a** an email	**b**	a photo	**c**	a text
6	send	**a** an email	**b**	a photo	**c**	social media
7	leave	**a** a message	**b**	a comment	**c**	an app
8	use	**a** my music	**b**	my computer	**c**	my watch
9	watch	**a** a comment	**b**	a movie	**c**	a video
10	buy	**a** my family	**b**	apps	**c**	a cell phone

B **Look at 1–6. Write *on,* or write *X* where *on* is not correct.**

1 ______________ the internet
2 ______________ my phone
3 ______________ my room
4 ______________ the tablet
5 ______________ my laptop
6 ______________ China

2 GRAMMAR: Simple present *yes/no* questions with *I, you, we*

A **Complete the questions with the verbs.**

1 ___Do you have___ a laptop? (you/have)
2 ______________ social media apps? (you and your friends/love)
3 ______________ your family? (you/call)
4 ______________ photos on social media? (I/post)
5 ______________ a new tablet? (you and your family want)
6 ______________ videos on the internet? (you/watch)

B **Answer the questions in exercise 2A so they are true for you.**

1 ___Yes, I do. OR No, I don't.___
2 ______________
3 ______________
4 ______________
5 ______________
6 ______________

3 GRAMMAR AND VOCABULARY

A **Complete the sentences so they are true for you.**

1 I use my ______ laptop ______ at school.
2 I chat with ______________ on my phone.
3 I call my ______________ on my tablet.
4 We watch ______________ on my laptop at home.
5 I don't post ______________.
6 I read ______________ on the internet.
7 My friends and I send ______________.
8 I leave messages for my ______________.
9 I listen to ______________ on my phone.
10 I don't play ______________.

B **Read the words and then write questions and answers that are true for you.**

1 social media
Do you post comments on social media? ______ Yes, I do. OR No, I don't.
2 chat on your phone
______________ ______________
3 watch videos on TV
______________ ______________
4 send emails
______________ ______________
5 leave voice messages
______________ ______________
6 call your friends
______________ ______________

4.3 WHAT ABOUT YOU?

1 FUNCTIONAL LANGUAGE: Continuing a conversation

A **Put the conversation in the correct order.**

Juan	Yes, and I send thank-you emails to my friends.	____
David	No. I use email or social media.	____
Juan	Do you send text messages to your parents?	1
David	Do you send thank-you cards, too?	____
David	Yeah, I send birthday cards to my grandparents. How about you?	____
Juan	What about cards?	____
Juan	Yes, I send cards, too. I like cards with interesting pictures.	____

2 REAL-WORLD STRATEGY: Showing you are listening

A **Circle the best response to complete the conversations.**

1 **A** I love Instagram.
B *Yeah, me too. / How about you?*
A It's really cool.

2 **A** Do you use Snapchat?
B *Right. / No. How about you?*
A I love it.

3 **A** I use video chat a lot. What about you?
B *Yeah. / OK.*
A I like video chat.

4 **A** This is a great new app!
B *Right. / No.*
A I really like it.

5 **A** I buy music on the internet.
B *Yeah. / I like email.*
A It's good.

6 **A** Do you watch movies on your cell phone?
B *No, I don't. / Right.*
A I do. It's great.

3 FUNCTIONAL LANGUAGE AND REAL-WORLD STRATEGY

A **Complete the sentences. Follow the instructions in parentheses ( ).**

Ana I don't call my family on my cell phone.

Sam Really?

Ana Yeah, it's expensive.

Sam Yes, it is. 1 Do you use video chat? ________ (*Ask a question to start a new topic.*)

Ana Sorry, I don't understand. What is a video chat?

Sam You talk with your friends with video. I use video chat on the internet. It's free.

Ana 2 ________________ (*Show Ana is listening.*)

Sam We have an app.

Ana 3 ________________ Is Skype an app for video chats? (*Show Ana is listening.*)

Sam Yes, it's one app. I use WhatsApp, too.

Ana 4 ________________ (*Ask a question to start a new topic.*)

Sam I don't use email. I send texts.

Ana 5 ________________ (*Ask for a response about the topic.*)

Sam Oh, no. I don't text my family. I call them. 6 ________________ (*Ask for a response about the topic.*)

Ana I send emails to my parents. They don't like texts.

Sam Really?

4.4 GREAT! FIVE STARS

1 LISTENING

A 4.01 LISTEN FOR DETAILS **What do Mai and Jonas talk about? Circle the correct answer.**

1 video games
2 apps
3 product reviews
4 their favorite things

B 4.01 LISTEN FOR SUPPORTING DETAILS **Listen again. Check (✓) what Mai and Jonas say about their phones.**

	Mai	Jonas
1 loves the phone	✓	____
2 doesn't like the phone	____	____
3 has great apps	____	____
4 reads email	____	____
5 sends text messages	____	____
6 posts comments on social media	____	____
7 doesn't like the music app	____	____

2 GRAMMAR: *a/an*; Adjectives before nouns

A **Circle *a* or *an* in each sentence.**

1 We don't have *a* / *an* apartment.
2 We have *a* / *an* house.
3 She has *a* / *an* app for video chat.
4 You don't have *a* / *an* email address.
5 He doesn't use *a* / *an* tablet.

B **Make one long sentence from the two short sentences.**

1 It's a book. It's interesting. *It's an interesting book.*
2 I have a TV. It's expensive. ____________________
3 It's a card. It's great. ____________________
4 Are they games? Are they boring? ____________________
5 It's a movie. It's old. ____________________
6 It's a smartwatch. It's cool. ____________________

3 WRITING

A **Match the beginning of the sentence (1–6) with the end of the sentence (a–f).**

1 I like to listen to music, but	____	a	my friends use it.
2 I don't like social media, but	____	b	it's old.
3 I don't have a smartwatch because	f	c	I don't like earphones.
4 We watch videos on the laptop, but	____	d	it takes good pictures.
5 I don't use my laptop because	____	e	we want a new TV.
6 We like the camera because	____	f	they're really expensive.

B **Read the thank-you email. Add two exclamation points.**

Reply Forward

Dear Aunt Martha and Uncle Tom,
Thank you for the smartwatch. It's really cool.
I video chat with my parents and my friends.
Love,
Dana

C **Write a thank-you email for a gift.**
Say why you like the gift.

CHECK AND REVIEW

Read the statements. Can you do these things?

UNIT 4	Mark the boxes. ☑ I can do it. ? I am not sure. **I can …**	If you are not sure, go back to these pages in the Student's Book.
VOCABULARY	☐ **use technology words.**	page 34
	☐ **use verbs for using technology.**	page 36
	☐ **use *on* before certain words.**	page 36
GRAMMAR	☐ **use the simple present with *I*, *you*, and *we*.**	page 35
	☐ **use *yes/no* questions in the simple present with *I*, *you*, and *we*.**	page 37
	☐ **use *a/an* and adjectives before nouns.**	page 40
FUNCTIONAL LANGUAGE	☐ **ask questions to develop a conversation.**	page 38
	☐ **show I am listening.**	page 39
SKILLS	☐ **write a thank-you email.**	page 41
	☐ **use exclamation points.**	page 41

UNIT 5 MONDAYS AND FUN DAYS

5.1 PLAY OR FAST-FORWARD?

1 VOCABULARY: Days and times of day; everyday activities

A **Look at the words in the box. Write the words.**

~~in the morning~~	~~on Saturday~~	play soccer	work	on Wednesday	run
go out	on Thursday	in the evening	on Friday	at night	
in the afternoon	on Monday	on Tuesday	study	on Sunday	

Activities							
Days of the week	on Saturday						
Times	in the morning						

B **Read about Rhea and Jon. Complete the sentences.**

	Monday	Tuesday	Wednesday	Thursday	Friday	Saturday	Sunday
Rhea	morning: work	morning: work	morning: work evening: go out with Teri and Jon	morning: work	morning: work night: go out with Jon	morning: run with Jay	afternoon: go out with family
Jon	morning: study evening: work	morning: study evening: work	morning: study evening: go out with Teri and Rhea	morning: study evening: work	morning: work night: go out with Rhea	morning: play soccer	morning: play soccer

1 Rhea works in the morning from Monday to Friday.
2 On Saturday, Rhea ________________.
3 On Wednesday evening, Rhea ________________.
4 Rhea ________________ with her family ________________.
5 Jon ________________ in the morning from Monday to Thursday.
6 On the weekend, Jon ________________.
7 Jon works ________________.
8 On Friday night ________________.

2 GRAMMAR: Simple present statements with *he, she* and *they*

A **Complete the sentences with affirmative (+) verbs.**

1 Javier and Allie play soccer on Friday. Allie plays on Saturday, too.
2 Maddie and Nat go to class on Monday night. Alma ________________ on Wednesday night.
3 Jay, Laura, and Terry have fun on weekends. Their brother ________________ fun on weekdays.

4 My wife wants a refrigerator. My children ______ a TV.
5 My friends and I study before class. Hugo ______ after work.
6 Miranda works in the morning. Eric and Alan ______ in the afternoon.

B **Complete the sentences with negative (–) verbs.**

1 I don't study in the morning. My friends *don't study* at night.
2 Juliana and Roberta don't have free time on Friday. Max ______ free time on Thursday.
3 Robin doesn't run in the morning. Her friends ______ in the afternoon.
4 Mr. and Mrs. Cho don't go out on the weekend. Their son ______ out on weekdays.
5 I don't watch TV. My cousin ______ videos.
6 Chen and Juan don't like coffee. Sam ______ tea.

C **Read the words. Then make correct sentences.**

1 ☐ my laptop. / use / never / I — *I never use my laptop.*
2 ☐ and / hardly ever / soccer. / my friends / I / play ______
3 ☐ My sister / at / studies / usually / night. ______
4 ☐ go out / I / night. / Friday / often / on ______
5 ☐ at / on / always / are / the weekend. / They / home ______

3 GRAMMAR AND VOCABULARY

A **Complete the sentences about what you do and don't do in the week. Make them true for you.**

1 I always *sleep in the morning* on the weekends.
2 I usually ______ in the evening.
3 I often ______ in the morning.
4 I sometimes ______ on Monday afternoon.
5 I hardly ever ______ on Sunday.
6 I never ______.

B **Read about what Katya and Lucas do. Then write five affirmative (+) and negative (–) sentences.**

	Katya	Lucas
go out on Friday night	*never*	*usually*
have fun on weekends	*often*	*never*
play soccer	*never*	*hardly ever*
watch soccer games on Saturday	*sometimes*	*never*
run early in the morning	*usually*	*usually*
study at night	*usually*	*never*
study in the morning	*hardly ever*	*usually*
work on Saturday and Sunday	*never*	*always*
work on Friday night	*always*	*never*

1 *Katya doesn't go out on Friday night. She always works on Friday night.*
2 ______
3 ______
4 ______
5 ______
6 ______

5.2 LISTEN TO YOUR BODY CLOCK

1 VOCABULARY: Telling the time

A **Look at the pictures and write the times.**

1 ___It's two thirty.___ 2 ____________ 3 ____________

4 ____________ 5 ____________ 6 ____________

B **Put the sentences in order for you. Then write the times for you. Write *X* for activities you do not do.**

____ I drink coffee ____________

____ I go to class ____________

____ I go to work ____________

____ I eat breakfast ____________

__1__ I get up ___at 7:00 a.m.___

____ I go to bed ____________

____ I drink tea ____________

____ I have dinner ____________

____ I eat lunch ____________

2 GRAMMAR: Simple present questions

A **Read the answers. Then complete the *yes/no* questions and information questions.**

1 **A** ___Does___ your family ___have___ a big lunch on Saturday?

B No, my family doesn't have a big lunch on Saturday.

A ___What does___ your family have on Saturday?

B They have a big breakfast on Saturday.

2 **A** ____________ you ____________ late on Monday?

B No, I don't get up late on Monday.

A ____________ you get up late?

B I get up late on Sunday.

3 **A** ____________ your best friend ____________ basketball?

B No, he doesn't play basketball.

A ____________ your best friend play?

B He plays soccer.

4 A ______________ your teacher ______________ on weekends?
B No, she doesn't work on weekends.
A ______________ your teacher work?
B She works from Monday to Friday.

5 A ______________ you ______________ lunch at school?
B No, I don't eat lunch at school.
A ______________ you eat lunch?
B I eat lunch at home.

6 A ______________ your friends ______________ to bed late on Friday and Saturday?
B Yes, they go to bed late on Friday and Saturday.
A ______________ your friends go to bed on Friday and Saturday?
B They go to bed after midnight.

B **Look at the *yes/no* questions in exercise 2A. Write true answers.**

1 *Yes, we do.* OR *No, we don't.*
2 ______________
3 ______________
4 ______________
5 ______________
6 ______________

3 GRAMMAR AND VOCABULARY

A **Write six questions. Use each word in column A.**

A	B	C
What What time When Where Do Does	you your parents your mother your father your brother(s) and sister(s) your brother(s) your sister(s) your best friend your friends your teacher	do on weekends drink coffee / tea eat breakfast / lunch / dinner get up go to bed / classes / work go out have breakfast / lunch / dinner have fun play basketball / games / soccer study work

1 *Do your parents go out on the weekend?* OR *When do your parents go out?*
2 ______________
3 ______________
4 ______________
5 ______________
6 ______________
7 ______________

B **Answer the questions in exercise 3A for you.**

1 Do your parents go out on the weekend? *No, they don't.*
When do your parents go out? *They go out on their birthdays.*

5.3 ME, TOO

1 FUNCTIONAL LANGUAGE: Showing you agree and have things in common

A **Circle the correct responses.**

1 You study a lot.
 a Yeah, I know.
 b Me, neither.
 c Me, too.

2 Sports are great.
 a Yeah, I know. They are boring.
 b That's true. I hardly ever watch them.
 c I agree. I play a lot of sports.

3 A good job is important.
 a I agree. What about you?
 b That's true.
 c Me, too.

4 I don't work on weekends.
 a Me, neither. But I work on Friday.
 b Me, too. I work on Saturday morning.
 c I agree. I don't work on weekends.

B **Val and Mateo have a lot in common. Complete Mateo's sentences with *Me, too* or *Me, neither*.**

1 **Val** I love my phone. **Mateo** Me, too.
2 **Val** I don't get up early on weekends. **Mateo** ______
3 **Val** I don't eat a big breakfast. **Mateo** ______
4 **Val** I run in the evening. **Mateo** ______
5 **Val** I go to bed late. **Mateo** ______
6 **Val** I don't drink tea. **Mateo** ______

2 REAL-WORLD STRATEGY: Short answers with adverbs of frequency

A **Answer the questions for you. Use adverbs of frequency.**

1 **A** Do you run?
 B Sometimes.
2 **A** Do you eat breakfast?
 B ______
3 **A** Do you go out on weekends?
 B ______
4 **A** Do you study in the morning?
 B ______
5 **A** Do you go to bed at 10 o'clock?
 B ______
6 **A** Do you play video games?
 B ______

3 FUNCTIONAL LANGUAGE AND REAL-WORLD STRATEGY

A **Complete the conversation. Use the words in the box.**

agree	~~do~~	hardly ever	neither
sometimes	too	true	yeah

Min-seo [1] ___*Do*___ you watch TV on the weekend?
David [2] ________. I think it's boring.
Min-seo I [3] ________. I only watch sports on TV.
David What sports do you watch?
Min-seo All sports. I love sports.
David Me, [4] ________.
Min-seo Do you play sports?
David No. I don't have a lot of free time.
Min-seo Me, [5] ________.
David But I run every day before dinner. Exercise is good.
Min-seo That's [6] ________.
David How about you? Do you run?
Min-seo [7] ________. My friends and I run on the beach on the weekend.
David The beach is a great place to run.
Min-seo [8] ________, I know.

B **You meet a new person. You have a lot in common. Write a conversation. Ask about their free time activities. Use adverbs of frequency and words from the box in exercise 3A.**

5.4 A HAPPY LIFE

1 READING

A **SKIM** **Skim the magazine article. Then check (✓) the correct title.**

____	**Title One:**	All Play and No Work Is Not Good for Children
____	**Title Two:**	All Work and No Play Is Not Good for Children
____	**Title Three:**	All Sleep and No Play Is Not Good for Children

Eva is 12 years old. She gets up at 6:00 a.m. and studies for an hour before breakfast. She goes to school at 8:30 and comes home after 6 o'clock. She eats lunch at school and studies for an hour before her afternoon classes. After school on Monday, she has guitar lessons. After school on Tuesday and Thursday, she has Chinese class. After dinner, she plays the guitar and studies from 7:00 to 10:30. She usually goes to bed at 11:00 p.m.

What does Eva do on weekends? Does she have fun? She gets up at 8:00 or 8:30. But after breakfast, she plays the guitar from 10 a.m. to 1 p.m. Then she eats lunch and reads a book. She doesn't have time for fun on the weekends! She goes to bed early – she's *always* tired!

Eva's a very good student, but is she happy? Are children happy when they don't play? Doctors say "no." Many children study in the evenings and on the weekends. This isn't good and the children aren't happy. Children want free time! Doctors tell parents: "Make sure your children work AND play!"

B **READ FOR DETAIL** **Read again. Complete the chart with three of Eva's weekday activities and the times for morning, afternoon, and evening/night.**

Morning activities	Afternoon activities	Evening/Night activities
1 *She gets up at 6:00 a.m.*	1 ____________	1 ____________
2 ____________	2 ____________	2 ____________
3 ____________	3 ____________	3 ____________

2 LISTENING

A 🔊 5.01 **LISTEN FOR SUPPORTING DETAILS** **Listen to the conversation. Write the numbers in the sentences.**

1 Dave: "I have *one/1* chocolate cookie before I go to bed."
2 Dave sleeps four or ____________ hours a night.
3 He drinks ____________ cups of coffee a day.
4 He eats ____________ meals a day.
5 He runs ____________ days a week.
6 He works at his desk ____________ or ____________ hours a day.

3 WRITING

A Read the headings (1–3) in the report. Use the sentences about Dave in exercise 2A to complete sentences a–f.

B REGISTER CHECK Write the sentences without *a.m.* or *p.m.*

1 We play basketball at 7 p.m.
We play basketball at seven in the evening.

2 I go to class at 8 a.m.

____

3 I study at 1 p.m.

____

4 I run at 6 a.m.

____

5 I go to bed at 11:30 p.m.

____

The "Good for You" Report

1 Great for you

a ______________________

b ______________________

2 Not good, but not bad for you

c *I have one chocolate cookie before I go to bed.*

d ______________________

3 Really bad for you

e ______________________

f ______________________

SCORE: ★★★★★

C Write your routines in the chart and make a "Good for You" report. Put a score at the end.

Great for you	Not good, but not bad for you	Really bad for you
SCORE ★★★★★		

CHECK AND REVIEW

Read the statements. Can you do these things?

UNIT 5	Mark the boxes. ☑ I can do it. ? I am not sure. **I can …**	If you are not sure, go back to these pages in the Student's Book.
VOCABULARY	☐ say days of the week and times of day.	page 44
	☐ tell the time.	page 46
	☐ use words for activities and routines.	pages 44 and 46
GRAMMAR	☐ use the simple present with *he/she/they*.	page 45
	☐ ask *yes/no* and information questions in the simple present.	page 47
FUNCTIONAL LANGUAGE	☐ show I agree or have things in common with someone.	page 48
	☐ answer questions with adverbs of frequency.	page 49
SKILLS	☐ write a report.	page 51

UNIT 6 ZOOM IN, ZOOM OUT

6.1 GOOD PLACES

1 VOCABULARY: Places in cities

A **Match the sentences (1–14) with the places (a–n).**

1 "I like animals."	n	a bookstore
2 "I want a new book."	____	b café
3 "I'm a doctor."	____	c college
4 "I love movies."	____	d hospital
5 "I'm a student, and I'm 20 years old."	____	e hotel
6 "I'm a student, and I'm 12 years old."	____	f mall
7 "I'm from the United States. I'm in Lima for five days."	____	g movie theater
8 "I love pictures by great artists."	____	h museum
9 "I want an expensive dinner."	____	i park
10 "I want coffee and a cookie."	____	j restaurant
11 "My children play with their friends after school."	____	k school
12 "I don't have milk or sugar at home."	____	l store
13 "I want some earphones, a camera, and tea."	____	m supermarket
14 "I want new furniture."	____	n zoo

2 GRAMMAR: *There's, There are; a lot of, some, no*

A **Complete the sentences about Amy's apartment. Use *there's* or *there are*.**

I live in a small town. In our town 1 ___there's___ a big park, but 2 ________ no zoo. 3 ________ a big supermarket, too, and 4 ________ three stores. My daughter goes to the school and my husband is a teacher at the school. 5 ________ an interesting bookstore. 6 ________ two really good restaurants!

B **Complete the conversation about Don's hotel. Use *no, a, some,* or *a lot of.***

Clara Do you like your hotel, Don?

Don Yes, I do. It's a big hotel! There are [1] ______________ rooms.

Clara Does the hotel have a restaurant?

Don Yes, it has [2] ______________ big restaurant. I eat breakfast in the restaurant every day.

Clara What about the restaurants near the hotel? Are they good?

Don Yes. There are [3] ______________ great restaurants near the hotel. Italian, Japanese, Spanish …

Clara And is your room good?

Don It's OK. There's [4] ______________ desk, [5] ______________ chair, and [6] ______________ big TV, but there's [7] ______________ sofa. It's not good!

3 GRAMMAR AND VOCABULARY

A **Write sentences about Ramón's city. Use *there's, there are, a, no, some,* and *a lot of.***

8 parks	2,000,000 people
3 hospitals	0 movie theaters
5 cafés	20 restaurants
1 hotel	0 good restaurants

1 There are a lot of parks.
2 ______________
3 ______________
4 ______________
5 ______________
6 ______________
7 ______________
8 ______________

B **Write six sentences about things you like and don't like about your city. Use *there's, there are, a, no, some,* and *a lot of.***

1 ______________
2 ______________
3 ______________
4 ______________
5 ______________
6 ______________

6.2 CITY LIFE, WILD LIFE

1 VOCABULARY: Nature

A **Look at the pictures and check (✓) the correct box.**

1 ☑ island, lake, snow
☐ river, flowers, hills
☐ forest, beach, mountains

2 ☐ island, grass, trees
☐ hills, plants, lake
☐ beach, flowers, ocean

3 ☐ desert, snow, forest
☐ forest, river, mountains
☐ hills, plants, flowers

4 ☐ plants, desert, mountains
☐ snow, trees, hills
☐ beach, grass, island

2 GRAMMAR: Count and non-count nouns

A **Circle the five mistakes.**

Count nouns	**Non-count nouns**
apartment	animal
artist	coffee
grass	furniture
milk	house
refrigerator	nature
restaurant	plant
sugar	snow

B **Complete the sentences. Use *a, an,* or *some*.**

1 I am ___an___ artist.
2 I have ________ house in a small city.
3 I don't have ________ large apartment.
4 There's ________ grass in my garden.
5 There's ________ table in the dining area.
6 There's ________ furniture in the house.
7 There's ________ plant in the living room.
8 There's ________ refrigerator in the kitchen.
9 There's ________ milk in the refrigerator.
10 There's ________ coffee next to the refrigerator.

3 GRAMMAR AND VOCABULARY

A **Complete the sentences. Use *There's* or *There are* and *a* or *a lot of*.**

1 ___There are___ ___a lot of___ hills in my city.
2 ________ ________ very tall tree.
3 ________ ________ grass.
4 ________ ________ flowers.
5 ________ ________ lake.
6 ________ ________ plants.
7 ________ ________ mountain.
8 ________ ________ snow on the mountain.

B **Look out your window. What do you see? Write <u>six</u> sentences. Use *There is* or *There are*. Use *a, an, no, some*, or *a lot of*.**

6.3 IS IT NEAR HERE?

1 FUNCTIONAL LANGUAGE: Asking for and giving directions

A **Complete the conversation. Use the words in the box.**

block	near	this	turn right	~~where's~~

Marina Excuse me. [1] *Where's* Central Hospital?
Ricky It's on Milk Street.
Marina Is [2] ________ Milk Street?
Ricky No, it isn't. This is Garden Street.
Marina Is Milk Street [3] ________ here?
Ricky Yes, it is. Turn left here. Then [4] ________ on Park Street. Go one [5] ________. The hospital is on the left.

2 REAL-WORLD STRATEGY: Checking information

A **Complete the conversation.**

Martin Excuse me. Where's the supermarket?
Althea Go one block and turn right on Good Street.
Martin [1] *So, go one block and turn right on Good Street.*
Althea Yes. Turn right on Good Street. [2] ________
Martin So, after the bookstore, turn right again.
Althea Yes. That's Second Street. Go two blocks and turn left.
Martin [3] ________
Althea That's right. That's Market Street. [4] ________
Martin So, the supermarket is on Market Street, on the right.
Althea Yes.

3 FUNCTIONAL LANGUAGE AND REAL-WORLD STRATEGY

A **Look at the map and read the conversation. Complete the directions.**

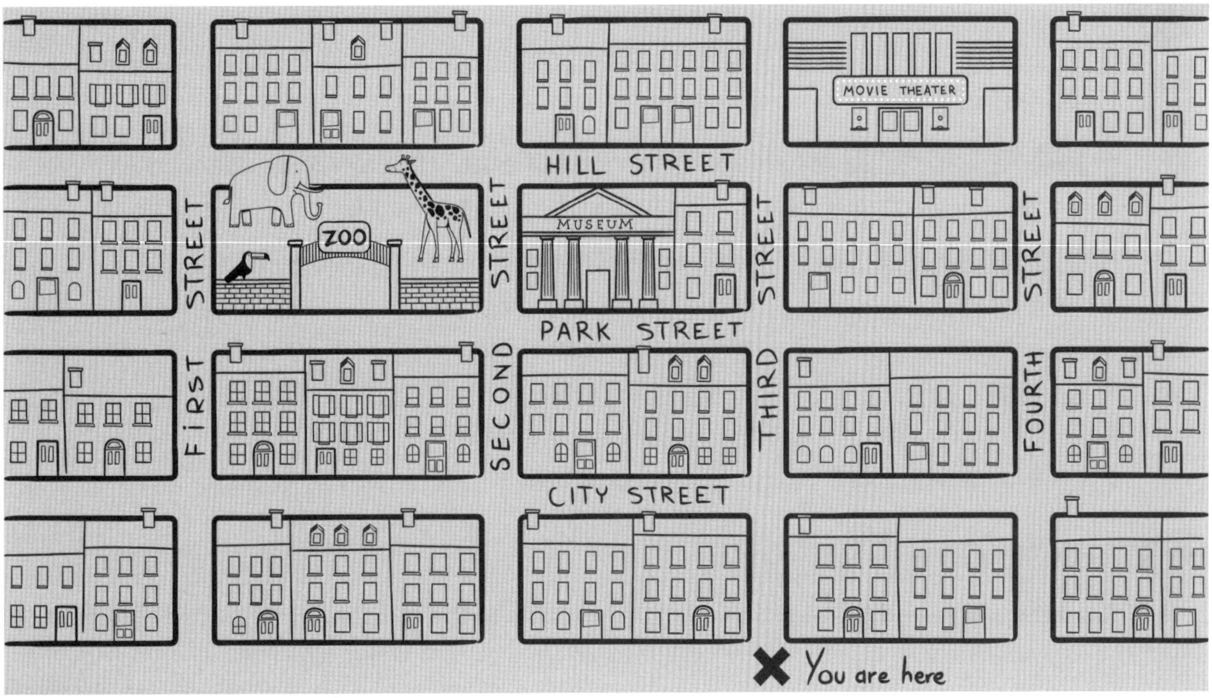

Rodrigo Excuse me. Where's the zoo?
Ji-young The zoo?
Rodrigo Yes, the zoo. Is it near here?
Ji-young Yes. It's near here. It's on ________________ Street. Walk down Third Street. Go two blocks and then turn ________________.
Rodrigo So, go two blocks and then turn left. Is that the zoo?
Ji-young No, that's Park Street. Go one ________________. It's on the right.
Rodrigo So, go one block, and it's on the ________________?
Ji-young Yes. The zoo is on the right.
Rodrigo Great. Thanks.
Ji-young You're welcome.

B **You are at the zoo. Write directions from the zoo to the movie theater.**

C **You are at the movie theater. Write directions from the movie theater to the museum.**

6.4 A FOREST IN THE CITY

1 LISTENING

A 6.01 LISTEN FOR GIST **Where are the people? Check (✓) the correct answer.**

_____ in a movie theater _____ in a car _____ in a house

B 6.01 LISTEN FOR EXAMPLES **Listen again. Check (✓) the things the people see.**

1 ☑ a building
2 ☐ a garden
3 ☐ a park
4 ☐ a green building
5 ☐ a garden on a wall
6 ☐ plants on a wall
7 ☐ flowers on a wall
8 ☐ trees on a wall
9 ☐ animals on a wall
10 ☐ grass on a wall

2 READING

A **Read the article and the questions. Are the answers to the questions in the article? Check (✓) *Yes* or *No*.**

What are vertical gardens?

They are gardens on walls. Vertical gardens are on tall buildings and on short buildings, and they are inside buildings and outside buildings. These gardens have a lot of different plants. Some vertical gardens have 400 different plants! Vertical gardens are good for cities and they are good for people. There are vertical gardens in many cities in the world. Sydney, Singapore, and Mexico City have vertical gardens. What about *your* city? Does it have a vertical garden?

	Yes	No
1 What is a vertical garden?	☐	☐
2 Who makes vertical gardens?	☐	☐
3 Is a vertical garden expensive?	☐	☐
4 Are gardens good for people?	☐	☐
5 What are the names of some cities with vertical gardens?	☐	☐

3 WRITING

A **Read the words and make sentences.**

1 nice / have / parks / some / we / small — *We have some nice small parks.*
2 there / beautiful / trees / some / tall / are ______
3 of / are / lot / flowers / small / interesting / there / a ______
4 plants / big / are / there / a / of / nice / lot ______
5 tall / the / has / trees / great / some / park ______

B **Read the fact sheet and add *very* to make the adjectives strong.**

- Via Verde is a busy road in Mexico City.
- There are 30 kilometers of vertical gardens next to the road.
- Via Verde is a big vertical garden. There are 700 small gardens in it.
- There are a lot of interesting plants in the gardens.
- People like the plants and flowers on Via Verde.
- People in Mexico City think the vertical gardens are interesting.
- Vertical gardens are important to Mexico City.

C **Write a fact sheet about an interesting place you know. Use *very*. Do <u>not</u> use contractions.**

CHECK AND REVIEW

Read the statements. Can you do these things?

UNIT 6	Mark the boxes. ☑ I can do it. ? I am not sure. I can …	If you are not sure, go back to these pages in the Student's Book.
VOCABULARY	☐ use words for places in cities. ☐ use words for places in nature.	page 54 page 56
GRAMMAR	☐ use *There's/There are* with *a/an, some, a lot of, no.* ☐ use count and non-count nouns.	page 55 page 57
FUNCTIONAL LANGUAGE	☐ ask for and give directions. ☐ check information by repeating.	page 58 page 59
SKILLS	☐ write a fact sheet. ☐ use *very* correctly.	page 61 page 61

EXTRA ACTIVITIES

1 TIME TO SPEAK People from history

A **Go online. Find information about the people in the photos in Student's Book lesson 1.5 (page 10).**

- Find the people's jobs.
- Find one other piece of information.
- Write one sentence for each person. Say the job and one other thing.

2 TIME TO SPEAK What's true for me

A **Write sentences that are true for you and your friends.**

- Write how you and your friends are the same.
- Write how you are different.

B **Read your sentences to your class.**

3 TIME TO SPEAK A new home

A **Go online. Find something to buy for your home.**

B **Write three sentences about it. For example:**

- It's an interesting color.
- It's cool.
- It's good for my desk.

C **Read your sentences to your class.**

4 TIME TO SPEAK Playlists

A **Go online. Find a song in English. Are the verbs from Unit 4 in the Student's Book in the song?**

B **Circle *a* or *an* in the words of the song.**

5 TIME TO SPEAK Life = 5 + 2

A **Go online and research the work week in three countries.**

B **How many days do people work? How many hours do they work?**

C **Read your sentences to your class.**

6 TIME TO SPEAK A good place to live

A **Look online for pictures of a city in your country or another country.**

B **Plan your visit. What places do you want to see in the city? What do you want to do in the city?**

C **Write about the things you want to do in the city.**

NOTES

NOTES

The authors and publishers acknowledge the following sources of copyright material and are grateful for the permissions granted. While every effort has been made, it has not always been possible to identify the sources of all the material used, or to trace all copyright holders. If any omissions are brought to our notice, we will be happy to include the appropriate acknowledgements on reprinting and in the next update to the digital edition, as applicable.

Key: B = Below, BR = Below Right, CL = Centre Left, CR = Centre Right, T = Top, TL = Top Left, TR = Top Right.

Photo
All photos are sourced from Getty Images.

p. 2: David Arky; p. 3, p. 8 (CL), p. 27 (BR), p. 33: Westend61; p. 4, p. 22: Caiaimage/Sam Edwards; p. 5, p. 14: Caiaimage/Tom Merton; p. 6: John Borthwick/Lonely Planet Images; p. 7: Eric Audras/ONOKY; p. 8 (TL): Tetra Images/Brand X Pictures; p. 8 (TR): Jose Luis Pelaez/Iconica; p. 8 (CR): Kali9/iStock/Getty Images Plus; p. 11 (TR): Juanmonino/E+; p. 11 (B): Tom Merton/Caiaimage; p. 12 (old): Sally Anscombe/Moment; p. 12 (boaring): LWA/Dann Tardif/Blend Images; p. 12 (short): Paperboat/E+; p. 12 (shy): Imagenavi; p. 12 (funny): Hollie Fernando/DigitalVision; p. 12 (reading): Tim Hall/The Image Bank; p. 12 (friendly): Robert Daly/OJO Images; p. 12 (couple): Ken Chernus/Photodisc; p. 12 (kid): Emma Kim/Cultura; p. 12 (boy): William King/Taxi; p. 12 (woman): Blend Images - Hill Street Studios/Brand X Pictures; p. 15 (TR): Tim Macpherson/Cultura; p. 15 (B): PhotoAlto/Sigrid Olsson/PhotoAlto Agency RF Collections; p. 16: Sjenner13/iStock/Getty Images Plus; p. 19: Nikada/E+; p. 20 (photo 1): Johner Images; p. 20 (photo 2): ExperienceInteriors/iStock/Getty Images Plus; p. 20 (photo 3): Spaces Images/Blend Images; p. 20 (photo 4): Andreas von Einsiedel/Corbis Documentary; p. 21: AJ_Watt/E+; p. 23: Alena Gamm/EyeEm; p. 24 (photo 1): Jeremy Walker/Photographer's Choice; p. 24 (photo 2): Luiz Souza/NurPhoto/Getty Images; p. 26 (photo 1): Pagadesign/E+; p. 26 (photo 2): Alexander Spatari/Moment; p. 26 (photo 3): Hudiemm/E+; p. 26 (photo 4): alexsl/iStock/Getty Images; p. 26 (photo 5): Mrgao/iStock/Getty Images; p. 26 (photo 6): Howard Kingsnorth/The Image Bank; p. 26 (photo 7): Davidscar/iStock/Getty Images Plus; p. 26 (photo 8): Dave King/Dorling Kindersley; p. 27 (T): Oneclearvision/iStocK/Getty Images Plus; p. 28: Squaredpixels/E+; p. 29 (TR), p. 43: Hero Images; p. 29 (B): JGI/Tom Grill/Blend Images; p. 30: Tetra Images; p. 31: Deborah Kolb/Blend Images; p. 32 (CR): Topic Images Inc; p. 32 (B): Chris Ryan/Caiaimage; p. 35: Kali9/iStock/E+; p. 37: Shannon Fagan/Blend Images; p. 38: NicolasMcComber/E+; p. 40: Heide Benser/Corbis; p. 41: Sangfoto/iStock/Getty Images Plus; p. 42: Maremagnum/Photolibrary; p. 44 (TL): Rachid Dahnoun; p. 44 (CL): Joe daniel price/Moment; p. 44 (TR): Svjetlana/RooM; p. 44 (CR): Laszlo Podor/Moment; p. 45: Jhorrocks/iStock/Getty Images Plus; p. 46: Krakozawr/iStocK/Getty Images Plus; p. 48: Ferrantraite/Vetta; p. 49: David Bank/AWL Images.

Front cover photography by Arctic-Images/The Image Bank/Getty Images.

Illustrations by: Alejandro Mila (Sylvie Poggio Artists Agency) pp. 18, 47.

Audio production by CityVox, New York.

Corpus
Development of this publication has made use of the Cambridge English Corpus (CEC). The CEC is a multi-billion word collection of contemporary spoken and written English. It includes British English, American English, and other varieties. It also includes the Cambridge Learner Corpus, the world's biggest collection of learner writing, developed in collaboration with Cambridge Assessment. Cambridge University Press uses the CEC to provide evidence about language use that helps to produce better language teaching materials.

Our Evolve authors study the Corpus to see how English is really used, and to identify typical learner mistakes. This information informs the authors' selection of vocabulary, grammar items and Student's Book Corpus features such as the Accuracy Check, Register Check, and Insider English.